THE STORY OF THE CHARLOTTE HORNETS

Larry Johnson and Muggsy Bogues

Gordon Hayward

A HISTORY OF HOOPS

THE STORY OF THE

CHARLOTTE HORNETS

JIM WHITING

Kemba Walker

CREATIVE EDUCATION / CREATIVE PAPERBACKS

Published by Creative Education and Creative Paperbacks
P.O. Box 227, Mankato, Minnesota 56002
Creative Education and Creative Paperbacks are imprints of
The Creative Company
www.thecreativecompany.us

Design and production by Blue Design (www.bluedes.com)
Art direction by Rita Marshall
Production layout by Rachel Klimpel and Ciara Beitlich

Photographs by AP Images (Bill Haber, Marty Lederhandler, Winslow
Townson), Corbis (Tim Sharp), Getty (Andrew D. Bernstein, Bill Baptist, Lisa
Blumenfeld, Chuck Burton, Lou Capozzola, Tim DeFrisco, Mike Ehrmann,
Allen Einstein, Focus On Sport, Chris Graythen, Scott Halleran, Grant
Halvorson, Jacob Kupfeman, Streeter Lecka, Layne Murdoch, Joe Murphy,
Greg Nelson, Rick Osentoski, The Sporting News, Jamie Squire, Brian A.
Westerholt), Newscom (David T. Foster III/MCT, Albert Pena/Cal Sport
Media), Shutterstock (Brocreative, Valentin Valkov)

Library of Congress Cataloging-in-Publication Data
Names: Whiting, Jim, 1943- author.
Title: The story of the Charlotte Hornets / by Jim Whiting.
Description: Mankato, Minnesota : Creative Education/ Creative
    Paperbacks [2023] | Series: Creative Sports: A History of Hoops | Includes
    index. | Audience: Ages 8-12 | Audience: Grades 4-6 | Summary: "Middle
    grade basketball fans are introduced to the extraordinary history of
    NBA's Charlotte Hornets with a photo-laden narrative of their greatest
    successes and losses"-- Provided by publisher.
Identifiers: LCCN 2022007521 (print) | LCCN 2022007522 (ebook) | ISBN
    9781640266209 (library binding) | ISBN 9781682771761 (paperback) | ISBN
    9781640007611 (ebook)
Subjects: LCSH: Charlotte Hornets (Basketball team: 1988-2002)--History--
    Juvenile literature.
Classification: LCC GV885.52.C4 W553 2023 (print) | LCC GV885.52.C4 (ebook)
    | DDC 796.323/640975676--dc23/eng/20220518
LC record available at https://lccn.loc.gov/2022007521
LC ebook record available at https://lccn.loc.gov/2022007522

DeSagana Diop

CONTENTS

LEGENDS OF THE HARDWOOD

THE HORNETS BEGIN TO BUZZ

T he Charlotte Hornets began playing in the 1988–89 season of the National Basketball Association (NBA). General manager Carl Scheer knew his expansion team wouldn't top the league right away. His plan: make the playoffs in five years. After losing records in their first four seasons, Charlotte met Scheer's goal in 1992–93. They won 9 of their final 12 games to squeeze into the playoffs with a 44–38 record. One of the league's newest teams faced the Boston Celtics, one of the oldest. Hardly anyone was surprised when the Celtics easily won the first game. Many were surprised when the Hornets won Game 2 in double overtime. Playing at home for the first time in the series, the Hornets blew out Boston by 30 points in Game 3. Game 4 was almost the same for three quarters. Charlotte led by 18 points. Boston stormed back to take a one-point lead in the waning moments. Charlotte center Alonzo Mourning took an inbounds pass near the top of the key. He dribbled once to the right, then launched a long jump shot. He fell backward as the ball went into the net. His jubilant teammates swarmed over him. The Hornets became the first of the four most recent expansion teams to win a playoff series.

**ALEXANDER JULIAN (right)
FASHION DESIGNER
DESIGNED HORNETS' UNIFORMS**

George Shinn

THE LITTLE CITY
THAT COULD

In 1985, the NBA said it would add four
teams. Charlotte businessman George Shinn
put together a group to make a bid. Ten other
cities were interested. Many people thought
the Charlotte area was too small to support
a team. A newspaper writer noted, "The only
franchise Charlotte is going to get is one with
golden arches." That was a reference to the
McDonald's sign. Shinn wasn't discouraged.
"I had been on the bottom before," he
said. "Keep your faith, keep pushing, keep
believing." His presentation impressed the
owners. Charlotte was their top choice for a
new NBA team.

When Charlotte, North Carolina, received its franchise in 1988, owner George Shinn asked fan input in naming the team. The overwhelming choice was Hornets. The name dates back to the Revolutionary War. The British army came up against powerful fighters in the Charlotte area. British general Lord Cornwallis wrote to King George III, "This place is like fighting in a hornet's nest." A local minor league baseball team was also the Hornets. A team in the short-lived World Football League had used the name, too.

Before playing a single game, the Hornets made their mark on the NBA. Famed fashion designer Alexander Julian used teal as the uniform color. No other sports team had used it. Within a few years, it had become wildly popular. Teams at all levels were wearing teal. The Hornets were also the first NBA team with pinstripes on their uniforms. It set a trend.

Unfortunately, the new franchise's first game was unfashionably lopsided. The Hornets lost by 40 points to the Cleveland Cavaliers. They finished the year 20–62. Shooting guard Kelly Tripucka averaged more than 22 points a game. He led the team in scoring. Shooting guard Dell Curry provided instant offense off the bench.

The most memorable game came early in the season. Michael Jordan and the Chicago Bulls came to town. Jordan had helped nearby University of North Carolina win the 1982 college championship. In the basketball-crazy state, no one stood taller. The Hornets were underdogs. They were a collection of unwanted veterans and untested rookies. Wins were hard to come by. But on this day, the score was tied 101–101. Just a few seconds remained. Hornets power forward Kurt Rambis shoved a teammate out of the way after a missed shot. He tipped the ball into the basket as time ran out. "The place went nuts," Rambis said. "It went absolutely nuts." Team publicist Harold Kaufman added, "In terms of something that transformed a city and a franchise and set it on a certain path, I think that one game did that more than anything else."

LEGENDS OF THE HARDWOOD

DELL CURRY
SHOOTING GUARD
HEIGHT: 6-FOOT-4
HORNETS SEASONS:
1988–98

PRACTICE MAKES PERFECT

People who spend a lot of time playing basketball are often called "gym
rats." Dell Curry might be called a "barn rat." He grew up in a small town
in Virginia. His high school coach owned a farm. He gave Curry a key to the
barn. "It was just a beat-up barn floor with a basket, and I'd go in and shoot
for hours upon hours with no interruptions," Curry said. It paid off. He was a
McDonald's High School All-American in 1982 and NBA Sixth Man of the Year
in 1994. He retired as the Hornets' career leader in scoring. He has another
claim to fame. His son Steph plays with the Golden State Warriors and is one
of the greatest three-point shooters in NBA history.

ACCORDING TO PLAN

espite the losing record, Charlotte led the league in attendance. One reason was fan favorite point guard Tyrone "Muggsy" Bogues. At 5-foot-3, he was—and still is the shortest player in NBA history. Muggsy joined the team in 1988. The team's second year wasn't any better. The team finished 19–63. The Hornets showed modest improvement in 1990–91 with a 26–56 mark. The next year, they drafted power forward Larry Johnson. He and second-year guard Kendall Gill boosted the team. But a late-season slide resulted in a 31–51 record.

The team drafted Alonzo Mourning before the 1992–93 season. "Most rookies are a little intimidated coming into this league," said coach Allan Bristow. "'Zo' never backs down from anybody." Johnson became the first Hornets player chosen for the NBA All-Star Game. The young talent brimmed with confidence in the playoffs. After defeating the favored Celtics in the first round, the Hornets faced the top-seeded New York Knicks in the Eastern Conference semifinals. While the Hornets won just one of five games, the series was very close. Two losses were by four points. A third was by just two. The Hornets seemed to be on the rise.

But the injury bug stung the Hornets. Both Mourning and Johnson missed large chunks of the following season. They returned to help the team finish 41–41. Both players were healthy in 1994–95. Mourning averaged 21 points and 10 rebounds. He and Johnson played in the All-Star Game. Charlotte won 50 games for the first time. But the defending NBA champion Chicago Bulls swatted them out of the playoffs in the first round.

CONTINUED SUCCESS

The Hornets wanted to sign Mourning to a long-term contract. He didn't think the team offered enough money. Charlotte traded him. One player they got in return was small forward Glen Rice. He played in the All-Star Game. But the Hornets went just 41–41. Charlotte rebounded in 1996–97 behind Rice's sharpshooting. He averaged nearly 27 points. It was third-best in the league. Charlotte went 54–28, the best record in its history. But again the Hornets couldn't get out of the first round. They got swept by the Knicks.

Charlotte said goodbye to the popular Bogues the following season. Still, the team was almost as good as the previous year, winning 51 games. This time, the Hornets defeated the Atlanta Hawks in the first round of the playoffs. They fell to the Chicago Bulls in the conference semifinals. "We played hard, but we've still got a ways to go to be a champion," said coach Dave Cowens. An owners' lockout delayed the 1998–99 season. When it started, Charlotte struggled. Paul Silas replaced Cowens. As a player, Silas had a reputation as a tough rebounder and defender. He urged his players to take the same attitude. "Paul told us we could sit around and lick our wounds, or we could go out and make something of our season," said point/shooting guard David Wesley. The team responded. A late run brought their record to 26–24. It was just short of the playoffs.

Charlotte barreled into the following season. It went 49–33 before losing to Philadelphia in the first round of the playoffs. The Hornets won 46 games in 2000–01 and 44 the following season. Both times they easily won the first round but lost in the conference semifinals.

MUGGSY BOGUES
POINT GUARD
HEIGHT: 5-FOOT-3
HORNETS SEASONS:
1988—97

CHARLOTTE HORNETS

SIZE DOESN'T ALWAYS MATTER

When Muggsy Bogues was young, his friends thought he was too
short to play basketball. In desperation, he used milk crates as
baskets. He became a powerful defender. Finally, others saw his
talent. He starred in high school and college. Despite his small
stature, Bogues played in 14 NBA seasons. He notched 6,858 points,
6,726 assists, and 1,369 steals. Perhaps most remarkably, he blocked
39 shots. One block was against 7-footer Patrick Ewing who was
about to go up for a dunk. Instead, Muggsy stripped the ball.

DAVID WESLEY
POINT/SHOOTING GUARD
HEIGHT: 6-FOOT-1
HORNETS SEASONS:
1997–2002

NOT TOO LITTLE

David Wesley averaged nearly 21 points in his senior year at Baylor University. Still, scouts thought he was too small for the NBA. Wesley played a season in the Continental Basketball Association. He tried out with the New Jersey Nets and made the team. When Wesley joined Charlotte three seasons later, he had silenced the doubters. He averaged nearly 15 points a game with the Hornets. He also played solid defense. "It's the little guys who don't stuff a stat sheet from night-to-night who can really help bring a team together," said Elijah Edwards of FanSided. "Wesley was that type of guy. He could score, he could defend, and he could often be seen diving recklessly for loose balls."

HORNETS OUT, BOBCATS IN

When he brought the NBA to Charlotte, George Shinn was a local hero. But by 2000, he had serious legal problems. Fans turned against him. He became even less popular when he demanded that the city build a new arena at no cost to him. He said the team couldn't make enough money in the current space. They were last in attendance in 2001–02. The city refused. Shinn asked the league's permission to move the team to New Orleans. As part of the deal, the NBA promised Charlotte a new team. It would begin playing in 2004. Until then, there would be no pro basketball in Charlotte.

The new team's owner was Robert Johnson, co-founder of Black Entertainment Television (BET). Johnson was the first Black American billionaire. His first order of business was naming the team. Three finalists emerged: Bobcats, Dragons, and Flight. As Johnson explained in his announcement of the winner, "No one wants to meet up with a bobcat in the woods, and that's the feeling we intend to create on the court with our team's new identity." There were other reasons for the nickname. The bobcat was a natural feline companion to the Carolina Panthers, Charlotte's professional football team. Many people thought the nickname also referred to Johnson's first name.

Boris Diaw

Before the 2004–05 season, the Bobcats selected several players from other teams. Coach Bernie Bickerstaff didn't want to spend money on older veterans. They would be gone after a couple of years. Instead, he focused on relative newcomers to the league such as forward Gerald Wallace. He had spent most of his three years with the Sacramento Kings on the bench. "We're a bunch of young guys who got overlooked," said Wallace, nicknamed "Crash" for his aggressive playing style. "All you want in this game is a chance to show that you can play. This is our chance." Charlotte also had the second overall pick of the 2004 NBA Draft. It took forward/center Emeka Okafor. "Emeka is a great player, but we see more than that in him," said Bickerstaff. "We are counting on his intelligence, strength, and maturity to pull this young team together."

Gerald Wallace

n November, Charlotte defeated the defending champion Detroit Pistons 91–89. It was the first time in 33 years that an expansion team had defeated the reigning NBA champions. The next month, Okafor netted two last-second free throws as the Bobcats beat New Orleans 94–93. It was somewhat of a grudge match. "The fans wanted us to beat the [New Orleans] Hornets, and we sensed it meant a lot to the city," he said. Performances like that helped Okafor become NBA Rookie of the Year. Apart from these highlights, the team struggled. It ended with an 18–64 record.

Nevertheless, opposing teams respected the young Bobcats' effort. "Everybody said Charlotte was crazy because they went with all kids," said Houston Rockets coach Jeff Van Gundy. "But those kids fear no one and play their hearts out. They are only going to get better." They did. Charlotte won 26 games the following season. Then the team added one of the game's all-time legends. Michael Jordan became a part-owner. He also served as manager of basketball operations. The team continued to improve. The Bobcats won 35 games in 2008–09.

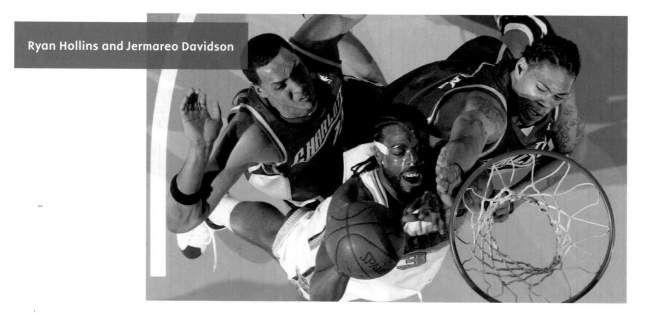

Ryan Hollins and Jermareo Davidson

EMEKA OKAFOR
POWER FORWARD/CENTER
HEIGHT: 6-FOOT-10
BOBCATS SEASONS:
2004–09

CHARLOTTE HORNETS

THE ART OF BLOCKING SHOTS

Emeka Okafor's first basketball skill was blocking shots. He averaged 7 blocks a game in high school and 4.3 in college. For most shots, he turned sideways so he could extend his right arm as high as possible. He faced would-be dunkers straight on, though. This helped him absorb some of the other person's weight. Blocking shots is risky. The force of the ball can smash one's fingers against the rim or backboard. Despite the potential dangers, Okafor rejected 10 New York Knicks shots in a game on January 12, 2007. His favorite block? "They were all good," he replied. "I love all my children."

Gerald Henderson

THE HORNETS RETURN

The Bobcats traded Okafor to New Orleans before the 2009–10 season. They received another shot-blocker, 7-foot-1 center Tyson Chandler, in return. Charlotte added fiery swingman Stephen Jackson. The Bobcats clawed their way to a 44–38 record. But the Orlando Magic swept them in the first round of the playoffs. Robert Johnson sold his interest in the team to Jordan. "Purchasing the Bobcats is the culmination of my post-playing career goal of becoming the majority owner of an NBA franchise," Jordan said. The Bobcats stumbled to a 34–48 mark the following season.

Then the bottom fell out. In the lockout-shortened 2011–12 season, Charlotte won only 7 of 66 games. The team's .106 winning percentage was the worst in NBA history. As NBA writer John Schuhmann noted, "When it comes to bad teams, some can't score … and some can't defend … The Bobcats can't do either." There was one bright spot. Rookie point guard Kemba Walker was selected for the Rising Stars Challenge during All-Star weekend.

In the 2012 NBA Draft, New Orleans beat out Charlotte for the top pick. New Orleans drafted future superstar Anthony Davis. Charlotte took defensive specialist small forward Michael Kidd-Gilchrist with the second pick. General manager Rich Cho said, "Out of the 17 years I've been in the NBA and involved with draft interviews and draft dinners, he's in the top five as far as that goes.

Stephen Jackson

Just a very, very high-character guy. Just a great, great work ethic, and he's only going to get better." Kidd-Gilchrist lived up to Cho's expectations. He was named to the NBA All-Rookie second team. He and Walker were named to the Rising Stars Challenge. Charlotte also added veteran guard Ben Gordon.

But even with the new talent, the team's bad luck continued. After a 7–5 start, the Bobcats had an 18-game losing streak. They finished 21–61. New coach Steve Clifford helped Charlotte improve to 43–39 and return to the playoffs the following year. The powerful Miami Heat swept the Bobcats. "Clifford has transformed the Bobcats' work environment, turning a wayward operation into competence," said sportswriter Adrian Wojnarowski. "They have an identity—defense, rebounding, and relentless player development amid a challenged roster."

Soon, the Bobcats added to that identity. The new owner of the New Orleans Hornets wanted to rename his team. He chose Pelicans. The brown pelican is Louisiana's state bird. Jordan asked the league to return the Hornets nickname and the history of the original Hornets to Charlotte. The league agreed. "Today is truly an historic day for our franchise, our city, and our fans as we mark the official return of the Charlotte Hornets," Jordan said.

Key injuries and other factors limited the Hornets in 2014–15. They finished 33–49. However, hopes ran high for the 2015–16 season. Charlotte drafted 2015 College Player of the Year power forward/center Frank Kaminsky and traded for shooting guard Nicolas Batum. Unfortunately, Kidd-Gilchrist injured his shoulder during a preseason game. He missed the entire season. Still, the Hornets enjoyed a winning record and a playoff berth. The Miami Heat bounced them in the first round. With Kidd-Gilchrist healthy, Charlotte was poised for another playoff appearance in 2016–17. But the Hornets finished 36–46. They matched that mark the following season.

Michael Kidd-Gilchrist

KEMBA WALKER
POINT GUARD
HEIGHT: 6-FOOT-0
BOBCATS/HORNETS
SEASONS: 2011–2019

SAVING HIS BEST UNTIL LAST

Kemba Walker was a high school and college All-American. Charlotte
had great expectations when they drafted him. He didn't disappoint. He
moved into the starting lineup in the middle of the 2011–12 season. He
became the first rookie with a triple-double that season. He started all
but four games in the next seven seasons. Walker had several noteworthy
accomplishments in his final season in Charlotte in 2019. He had his
highest points average (25.6). His 41 points in the season opener was a
franchise record for the first game. He scored a franchise-record 60 points
in a single game. He outscored the rest of the team combined. He became
the third Hornet to start in the All-Star Game.

CHARLOTTE HORNETS

The Hornets finished 39–43 in 2018–19. Walker left the team. Perhaps not coincidentally, Charlotte plunged to 23–42 the following season. Then play was suspended for several months due to the COVID-19 pandemic. When the games resumed, Charlotte was one of eight teams whose records weren't good enough to continue.

They improved to 33–39 in the 2020–21 season. One reason was rookie LaMelo Ball. He once scored 92 points in a high school game. He was named NBA Rookie of the Year. He averaged 15.7 points, 6.1 assists, and 5.9 rebounds. In early January, Ball became the youngest player in NBA history with a triple-double. He was 19 years and 140 days at the time.

Charlotte began the 2021–22 season among a group of teams hovering around the .500 mark. The Hornets finished with 11 wins in their final 17 games for a final 43–39 mark. It was their first winning season since 2015–16. Four-year veteran forward Miles Bridges became a full-time starter and averaged 20 points a game. Ball improved his averages per game to 19.9 points, 7.5 assists, and 6.7 rebounds. Charlotte earned a spot in the play-in tournament for the playoffs, but Atlanta crushed them, 132–103.

Charlotte fans are buzzing with excitement for their team. They continue to hope that a championship banner will soon hang in Charlotte's Spectrum Center.

LaMelo Ball

INDEX

Terry Rozier